EFFECTIVE
BUDGETING

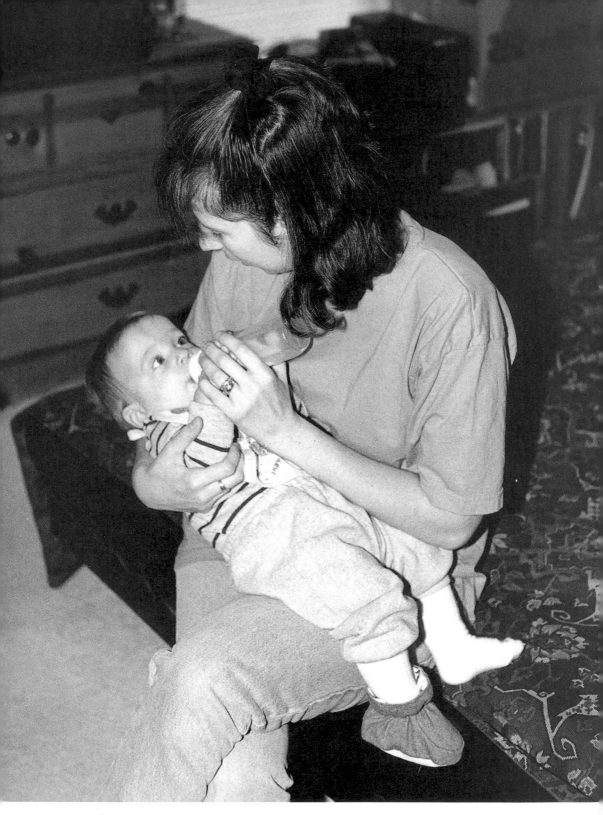

Effective budgeting can help you maximize and make good use of your earnings.

THE LEARNING-A-LIVING LIBRARY

High Performance Through
EFFECTIVE BUDGETING

Jane Hurwitz

THE ROSEN PUBLISHING GROUP, INC.
NEW YORK

Published in 1996 by The Rosen Publishing Group, Inc.
29 East 21st Street, New York, NY 10010

First Edition

Printed in the United States of America

Library of Congress Cataloging-in-Publication Data

Hurwitz, Jane.
    Effective budgeting / Jane Hurwitz.
        p.   cm. — (The learning-a-living library)
    Includes bibliographical references and index.
    ISBN 0-8239-2203-0
    1. Finance, Personal.   2. Budget, Personal.   3. Budget in
business.   I. Title.   II. Series.
HG179.H874   1996
332.024—dc20   95-39719
                                                           CIP

Contents

$15.95

Introduction

Is a budget like a diet? For many people, the idea of budgeting their money is about as appealing as dieting. But diets often tell you exactly what to eat, whereas budgets do not tell you exactly how to spend your money. And, unlike diets, budgets, for the most part, do not require extreme hunger or weigh-ins.

A budget is a plan that is used by both individuals and businesses. A personal budget is used to help you live as well as possible with the money that you have. In the business world, budgets help managers plan as well as possible for their companies and employees.

One of the largest budgets you hear about is that of the United States. It is called the federal budget, and it is designed to keep track of how the government spends its money and collects its income (taxes and other revenues).

Currently, the federal budget is unbalanced. This occurs in a budget when too much money is spent

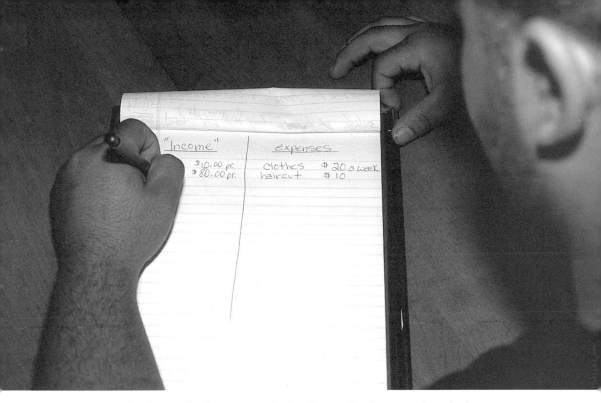

Keeping track of money received and spent is a key part of any budget.

or not enough money is received. The result of an unbalanced budget is that there is not enough money to pay all of the bills. In order to balance the federal budget, members of the Congress pass measures regulating how funds are spent.

It is obvious that a government needs to have a budget and keep track of how its money is spent and received. But what if you don't work and have only a small allowance from your parents? Even if you don't have a lot of money to keep track of, there are still good reasons to learn budgeting skills. A budget can help you in several ways:

1. It lets you know where and how your money is spent.

A recent study of fifteen hundred Americans found that 30 percent of those surveyed argued with their spouses about money. Thirty-eight percent of them worried about how money affected their marriages. Using a budget to keep track of money may decrease the worries of many people.

2. It helps you set aside money for bills.

Perhaps you currently receive an allowance from your parents or hold a part-time job after school. By budgeting the money that you receive each week, it may be possible for you to buy what you need, such as lunches, bus fare, and clothing, and still save for things you want, such as video games or expensive clothing.

3. It prepares you for unforeseen expenses.

Suppose you borrow a friend's in-line skates for the weekend. While skating, one of the wheels catches on a rock and pulls loose from the boot. Your friend agrees to wait while you have the wheel replaced, but where will you get the money to pay for the repair? Having a budget might help you to solve this problem. You would know how to rearrange your spending habits for a few weeks until you were able to save enough for the expense.

4. It makes it easier to save money.

Comparing families in industrialized countries,

Americans have one of the lowest rates of savings per household. A budget can't make a person save money, but it will increase the chances that money is spent in a wise fashion.

This book explains what budgets are and how they can work for you. It shows how to set up a budget now, no matter how small your income is. It shows how a budget can help you save money or plan a business. It examines basic budgeting concepts that can help you understand how to prepare and use more complex budgets. It discusses how to adjust budgets and use them for decision-making.

Few people will ever be responsible for a budget as large as the federal budget. But as your personal income and expenses grow over time, the ability to adjust and maintain a budget will enhance your personal and professional life.

Questions to Ask Yourself

The purpose of a budget, whether large or small, is to keep track of expenses and help you to spend and save wisely. 1) Why is the United States budget out of balance? 2) How can keeping a budget help you if your income is small? 3) Do you budget your allowance?

Keep track of the money you spend and categorize it by type of expense.

Budgeting Basics

MANY PEOPLE BELIEVE THAT CREATING AND USING a budget is about as much fun as going to the dentist. But using a budget doesn't have to be an anxiety-filled chore. Budgeting is a process of organization that allows people to meet their financial goals and dreams.

To begin organizing a budget, four basic steps are followed:

1. Setting financial goals.
2. Determining income.
3. Figuring expenses.
4. Subtracting expenses from income.

Setting Financial Goals

Jennifer wants to design a budget that will allow her to afford more expensive clothes. She doesn't necessarily *need* more expensive clothes; these are luxuries. Her friend Sloan hopes to create a budget that will help him avoid spending more money than he earns. Both of these people want to start using budgets, but each has a different goal.

A goal is a target that you set for yourself, something that you want to achieve. Goals can be large, such as saving for a car, or small, such as finding baby-sitting jobs to increase your income. Whether large or small, it is important to know your goal.

It may be helpful to think of your budget as a road map. It will mark the route from your current financial situation to a goal down the road. Like a map, there may be various paths that you can take to your goal. Studying your map, you can find the shortest one.

To understand where your budget can take you, first determine your goals in budgeting. Ask your parents about their financial goals. Do they use a budget? If not, why? Ask a few friends about their goals and how they plan to achieve them.

Next, divide your wishes into two groups: short-term goals and long-term goals. That will help you decide which to work on first. Short-term goals are smaller goals, things that can be accomplished in a short time, around six months to a year. Long-term goals are larger projects that take longer than a year to achieve.

Elaine

Elaine didn't know what to do. She was going to

Your financial goal may be related to a special interest or hobby.

turn sixteen in a few months, and her parents
wanted her to look for a part-time job. But Elaine
didn't want to work for a hamburger restaurant or
at the mall. She had a long-term goal of becoming a
photographer, and working at the mall wouldn't
take her toward her goal. After much thought,
Elaine devised a short-term goal that would please
her parents and also help her toward her goal of
becoming a photographer. By the time she turned
sixteen, she would find a part-time job related to
art or photography. Then her parents would be
satisfied, and she would still feel that she was making progress toward her career goal.

In the past, Elaine had baby-sat for families in her neighborhood. Using three of these families as references, she applied for an after-school job as an aide at a day-care center. With her good references, Elaine was accepted for the part-time position.

As an aide, Elaine plans to work with the older children on art projects, which might include taking pictures with disposable cameras. Elaine also hopes to use her own camera to take photographs while at work. Perhaps she will be able to create portraits of the children. Through setting and achieving a well-planned short-term goal, Elaine hopes to continue working toward her long-term goal of becoming a photographer.

Determining Income

A budget tracks how much money is received (income) and how much money is spent. To start using a budget, you must know how much money you have or will receive. Make a list of all the ways that you receive money. Even if you currently have only one source of income, it is important to list it. Your list may include:

- Allowance
- Gifts from relatives
- Baby-sitting fees
- Odd jobs such as car-washing or lawn-mowing

Most jobs involve budgeting in some way. For example, you may need to budget the supply of the product you are serving.

People who work or have multiple sources of income may want to create a worksheet to illustrate their sources of income. As your income grows, a worksheet can also help to track income that your savings creates, such as interest income.

The following worksheet was used by a married couple, Neal and Adriane, to track their income. Neal works as a cook for a small pizza restaurant, and Adriane is a dental hygienist. In addition to their salaries, they run a dog-walking service that supplies self-employment income.

Although they are both young, Adriane and Neal

Sources of Income Worksheet				
Earned Income	Neal	Adriane	Total	Monthly
Salary	$15,200	$14,800	$30,000	$2,500
Self-Employment	$500	$100	$600	$50
Investment Income				
Interest on Savings			$48	$4
Net Income				
	$15,700	$14,900	$30,648	$2,554

have a savings account that pays them monthly interest.

To simplify their recordkeeping, Adriane and Neal record their salary income after taxes and social security have been subtracted by their employers.

Since they want to use a monthly budget, they divide their total yearly income for each category by twelve. In this way they can calculate the monthly income column of their worksheet.

By recording their sources of income, Adriane and Neal know that their combined monthly income is $2,554.

How they spend this money depends in part on

Basic budgeting skills are essential to achieving short and long-term goals.

It is important to pay bills on time to avoid getting into debt.

the goals that they have set in the first step of the budget process. In their case, they have both a long-term and a short-term goal. They want to buy a house someday, but they also want to treat themselves to a vacation. They must try to budget for both of these goals.

Figuring Expenses

A budget can allow you to predict whether or not future expenses, or the amount of money that is spent each month, will increase or decrease. But before a budget can be set up, current expenses, or how money is spent today, must also be determined.

An easy way to determine current expenses is to record in a diary everything that you spend for a week. This "spending diary" may be nothing more than a slip of paper on which you record every purchase you make. At the end of the week, categorize all the purchases made. Then add expenses that occur once a month or once a year, such as rent or insurance. To determine how much you spend weekly on these fixed expenses, divide monthly expenses by four and divide yearly expenses by 52 (because there are approximately four weeks per month and 52 weeks per year). Even if you make a certain payment once a month, you should still account for it in your weekly budget.

Some sample categories of expenses are as follows:

- Entertainment, such as books, magazines, movies, videos, or compact discs.
- Food, such as school lunches and snacks.
- Transportation, such as bus or subway fare, gas money for car pools, or car payments (including insurance and repairs).
- Personal care, such as haircuts and cosmetics.
- Clothing.
- School/hobby supplies.

For example, Neal and Adriane earn a total of $2,554 per month. This is approximately $638.50

Checking out library books instead of buying books is a cost-cutting measure.

per week. This means that they have approximately $638.50 per week to spend on everything from rent to food to movie tickets. How much, they wonder, do they really spend per week? They decide to begin keeping a spending diary.

Monthly rent	$300 ($75 per week)
Food	$80 per week
Electric bill	$15 per week
Phone bill	$10 per week
Transportation	$20 per week
Total:	$200

Now that Adrinne and Neal have calculated their necessary expenses, they know that they have $438.50 left each week for optional expenses (entertainment, new clothing, savings, etc.).

A spending diary is a useful tool if you are just beginning a budget. It is also helpful if you have very few expenses. But it may not be enough if you have many expenses or want to create a monthly budget.

For larger budgets, such as monthly or yearly budgets, many people use a file folder with pockets. Each pocket is labeled with the name of the type of expense such as "Entertainment" or "Food." Receipts for items purchased during the month are filed in the appropriate pocket. If you buy something without receiving a receipt, simply file a note in the correct pocket. At the end of the month all expenses will be organized and ready to record in your budget.

Subtracting Expenses from Income

The fourth and final step in creating a budget is to subtract expenses from income. You have seen how Neal and Adriane have done this.

The result of this process will be either a positive number or a negative number. A positive result shows that income is larger than expenses, whereas a negative result shows that more money is being spent than earned. When the amount of income is greater than the amount of expenses, a budget is said to be "balanced."

Once You Have a Budget

Setting goals, figuring income, determining expenses, and finding a balance are the four steps for creating a beginning budget. But using these steps to create a budget is not the end of budgeting.

Budgeting is a tool. It is a means of figuring out how much you earn and how much you spend. Once you have determined your financial goals, added up your income, added up your expenses, and then calculated the difference between them, you can see how you spend your money. When you

Taking lunch to school can save several dollars a day.

understand how you spend your money, you can decide if you need to change your earning and spending habits in order to reach your financial goals. For Adriane and Neal, it was important to save money for a house and a vacation. Once they figured out their budget, they decided to set aside $50 per week for their long-term goal. A budget helped them to figure out how much they could save each month—in their case, about $200.

What if your budget amount at the end of the month is positive? That means that you earn more money than you spend. But, like Adriane and Neal, you may want to earn or save even more. Or you may decide that you are already earning enough money to buy something you have been hoping to buy.

What if your budget amount at the end of the month is negative—more money was spent than was earned? Can a budget with a negative balance be fixed?

The answer is yes. To change your budget from a negative balance to a positive balance means that you must increase how much you earn or decrease how much you spend. Your budget will help you decide if there are some expenses you can cut or if you need to find a way to earn more money. For instance, perhaps you can buy one compact disc instead of two each month. Or you might offer to rake leaves on the neighbor's lawn or get a part-time job.

Most negative budgets require a month or two of adjustments before they will come into balance. The basic remedies for unbalanced budgets are to reduce spending or increase income. "Budget adjustments" seem to be the hardest part of maintaining a budget. After all, no one likes to be told to spend less or find an extra job. But with practice and a little creativity, budget adjustments and using budgets in everyday life can be a simple way to achieve financial goals.

Questions to Ask Yourself

When setting up your own budget, it is important to decide on your goals and to determine your ability to maintain a balanced budget. 1) What are four steps to making a budget? 2) Why do you need a goal for budgeting? 3) How can a worksheet help in budgeting?

Budgeting at Home and School

THE FOUR STEPS OF BUDGETING CAN EASILY BE applied to personal situations. Depending on the goals set, a personal budget can help eliminate debt, increase spending power, or help to save money.

Eliminating Debt

The National Foundation for Consumer Credit estimates that 40 percent of middle-class families spend more than they make. It will not be unusual to find yourself in debt at some point in your life. Debt can arise from poor planning, excessive spending, or emergencies, but for most people, debt does not have to last forever.

Kenny

I started full-time employment with a travel agency six months ago, immediately after high school graduation. I love to travel and have worked for the agency during the past two summers. The agency specializes in tour packages to Europe, and I hope to get to go on a tour when I receive my first two-week vacation. I'm also studying German in the evenings at the community college. Someday, I hope to lead a group tour.

But now, after working for six months, I never seem to have any money at the end of the month, and I even owe some. Even though I have only one credit card, I never have enough money to pay the balance off at the end of the month. To meet my travel and career plans, I need to save money, not be in constant debt. Luckily, the student resource center at school put me in touch with the Consumer Credit Counseling Service (CCCS). The CCCS is a nationwide nonprofit agency that helps people reach their financial goals through counseling on spending habits and through the development of personal budgets.

Meeting with a credit counselor at CCCS, I discussed my financial plans and goals. I need to earn enough to pay for my community college classes and save for future travel in addition to covering my everyday expenses.

The counselor explained that before developing my savings plan, I need to eliminate the debt that is piling up each month. Before starting a budget to help save money, I have to create a budget to eliminate my debts. The counselor also suggested that I try to pay off my credit card balance over the next

Think about creative ways to save money, such as inviting friends to watch a movie instead of going out to a theater.

six months. To do so, I have to adjust my current budget either by increasing my income or decreasing my spending. After examining my income and expenses for each month, I made my decision.

To cut back on expenses, I will stop going to the movies every weekend. I usually see two movies per weekend, which can cost $20 if I also buy popcorn and a drink. At the end of the month, I will have an extra $80 to pay on my credit card account.

I also hope to increase my income. I plan to register at the community college as a tutor for beginning German language students. Even though the income probably won't be steady, it will help me to pay off my debt.

Often, the first step in eliminating debt is to reverse a negative balance on all credit cards as Kenny did. Credit cards are often easy to obtain, but they are not the same as free money.

Some hints for reducing credit debt in a personal budget:

- Put aside a certain amount of money every pay-day. Open a special bank account if necessary. Use this money for credit card debt reduction only.
- Place your credit cards in a place where they are not readily available.
- If you plan to charge an expensive item to a credit card and pay for it over a long period, choose a card with a low interest rate. Obtain a second credit card to use for purchases that will be paid off monthly. With this system, only the one large purchase will incur a monthly finance charge.

Spending Power

What if you have money left over after all monthly expenses are paid? Economists call this *discretionary income*, the amount of money left after all necessities (such as rent and food) are paid for. Having excess money indicates that the budget is balanced.

Another way to consider this extra money is as "spending power." Think of it as money that you have the power to spend (or save). It is money that you have a choice about. If you spend more money each month than you receive in income, your spending power is negative. If you make more money each month than you spend, your spending power is positive and you can decide what to do with the excess.

Spending power doesn't depend on how much money a person makes; it depends on what the person considers essential needs. As income grows, people often change what they consider essential. One person may consider a large-screen color television a necessity, whereas another would consider it a luxury. The way you define your wants and needs determines how much spending power is available in your budget. On the other hand, you may decide that you want to put some of your discretionary income into a savings account. Saving money allows spending power to remain high for each month. It can also heighten spending power in future months, because there will be surplus money in an account. That money will be earning interest, which also increases your spending power.

After setting up a basic personal budget, you may want to adjust it to increase your spending power. Just reevaluate what is necessary. There are two areas in a basic budget that may be adjusted: income and expense.

Spend Less

Many people have items in their budget that they can do without. Therefore, cutting back on expenses is often an easy way to increase spending power. Some ideas for cutting expenses can be started immediately:

- Take lunch to school or work instead of eating out.
- Buy less expensive clothing or shop at secondhand stores.
- Use a public or school library as an alternative to buying books, tapes, and compact discs, or renting videos.
- Before you go shopping, check the newspaper for special sales. And while you are out shopping, keep your eye out for unadvertised sales or markdowns.
- Buy items in large quantities. For example, buying at a wholesale store can often earn you a discount.
- Be smart about shopping in general. Comparing prices at different stores, bargain hunting, searching for rebates, and clipping coupons can all help cut down the amount of your expenses.

Earn More

Increasing income is the second method of increas-

Take public transportation or join a car pool to save money.

ing spending power. Often it takes longer to increase income than to decrease spending. Some options for increasing income in a personal budget:

- Find a part-time job. House-painting or baby-sitting may be possibilities.
- Ask for a raise in your current pay.
- Invest in more education or training. Vocational schools offer training programs that take less than four years to complete. Having a degree or specific training can increase your earning power.
- Take night classes at a community college. It will take more time to earn your degree going at night

than going full time, but you can make money as
you work toward it.

- Do odd jobs or landscaping in your neighborhood. There is always someone who is willing to
pay for someone else to mow their lawn, walk the
dog, or help with other chores.

Saving with a Budget

Increasing spending power alone will not turn a
personal budget into a budget that produces savings. The first aspect of the budgeting process, setting financial goals, must also be changed in order
to save money.

Roberta

I consider myself very lucky. I work ten hours a
week as a waitress. I have been working for four
months, and I always work the lunch shift on Satur-
days. I also work one night shift during the week,
but Saturday is when I work most of my hours. The
Saturday lunch shift doesn't generate much money
in tips but, until yesterday, those were the only
hours available to me, since I also attend high
school. But luck is on my side. One of the wait-
resses who works the Saturday night shift just quit,
and I will be able to switch to her position. The tips
will be more than double what I am used to; it's
just like getting a raise.

Even though earning money from tips is a bit erratic, I have a budget that I stick to. Each month I budget enough to pay for my lunches, bus fare, and ten dollars for a "clothing fund," which is really just a piggy bank. In a good month, I usually have a little money left, which I use to rent videos.

Now that I will be earning more money, I need to reevaluate my budget. Even though I didn't have much money at the end of the month when I worked the lunch shift, I was happy with my old budget. My short-term goals were met, and I felt that I had enough spending power to buy what I wanted. But now that I have the chance, I will change my budget and goals in two ways.

I am concerned about the treatment of animals and would like to be able to help the Humane Society. So I will adjust the expense side of my budget to include a $5 monthly donation to the Humane Society. That sounds small, but it will add up to $60 a year.

I will also add a long-term goal to my budget: saving for a used car. Until I have worked the new shift for a few months, I won't be certain of my average monthly wage. But I plan to save 5 percent of each paycheck in a "car fund." I estimate that I will need $3,000 to purchase a used car and one year's automobile insurance.

Since I am not sure about my total income yet, I

If you work at a job that generates income from tips instead of a regular salary, you may have to be especially careful about planning a budget.

will break my savings plan into two parts. For the first six months of my new budget, I will save 5 percent of each paycheck. At the end of six months, I will check the balance of my car fund and adjust my level if my savings are too low. I'd like to buy the car in three years when I turn twenty-one years old.

As a result of increased tips from her new shift, Roberta was able to adjust her financial goals and create a budget that included gifts to charity and savings for a long-term goal. Since Roberta had received an unexpected increase in her income, it

If you are part of a school activity that needs to advertise, you will need to budget for costs such as photocopying.

wasn't hard for her to adjust her personal budget to include savings as a long-term goal. But for many, it often isn't so easy to adjust a budget to include savings.

Putting Budgeting Skills to Use

Participation in school activities can be an opportunity to learn and practice budgeting skills. One consideration is that budgeting doesn't always just involve money. Money is one of many resources that may be allocated, or distributed. Budgeting may also involve allocating time, space, materials, and even people (human resources). For example, Arthur and his friend Willis want to start a club for students interested in in-line skating. Their initial budget looks like this:

Expenses	
Photocopying posters to advertise meetings	$10 per meeting
Refreshments at meetings	$10 per meeting

Other Needs
Room for meetings (classroom to be used for about one hour after school one night per week)
Club adviser (volunteer who can donate about two hours per month)

In this case, the budget is used to allocate expenses as well as space and human resources.

Arthur and Willis's budget is very simple and is easily approved by the principal. But their club becomes very popular, and they find that they want to do some more exciting activities that cost money. They draw up a budget for the new term.

Expenses	
Advertising costs	$10 per meeting
Refreshments at meetings	$10 per meeting
Rental of intructional skating video	$50
Demonstration and talk by professional skater	$30

Now the operation of the club is becoming more expensive. The principal is hesitant to approve the new budget. Arthur and Willis go back to the drawing board. They are committed to offering the new events. But they realize that to justify their new costs, they will have to show that they are spending less in other areas. They decide to have volunteers bring refreshments each week. That saves them $10 a week. They also decide to set up a phone tree to announce meetings rather than putting up posters. Arthur points out that this new system won't attract new members, since only old members will be on the phone list. Willis agrees. They still need some kind of advertisement. They settle on a general announcement over the school intercom, when other club meetings are announced. This won't cost them anything.

Arthur and Willis go back to the principal with their new budget. He is impressed by how they have reevaluated their original budget and scaled back costs. He approves the new budget.

Learning good budgeting skills to use at school and at home will help you improve the organizations in which you are involved. Just as important, budgeting skills can be applied to other areas. One of these areas is your job.

Questions to Ask Yourself

Budgeting, both at home and at school, can help you to use your money to get the things you want or need. 1) How can a budget help you to get out of debt? 2) Why can credit cards cause trouble if you don't keep a budget? 3) What is discretionary income?

Effective Budgeting on the Job

WORKING FOR AN EMPLOYER ALMOST ALWAYS requires the ability to understand a budget. People working in business use budgets for organizing resources and time. For example, a chef who manages a large kitchen in a restaurant uses a food budget to analyze the variables that go into producing a meal. The cost of producing meals (based on the price of ingredients), the price that can be charged per meal, and the expected volume of business are all analyzed. After considering all the variables, the chef will be able to tell if the restaurant will make a profit. If not, the chef will adjust one of the budget items (probably either the prices the restaurant charges or the cost of ingredients) until a profit can be made.

Other jobs use budgets to allocate people and time. Personnel managers assess the human resource needs of a company and adjust hiring after consulting a personnel budget. These managers have a budget that tells them what amount of

All kinds of jobs require budgeting skills, whether you work in an office or out of your home.

money is available for salaries. Even if a job is not at a managerial level, the ability to allocate money and resources is a basic skill needed to succeed in a job today.

Even as a part-time employee, you'll stand out if you have effective budgeting skills. Your boss may give you a project that requires the allocation of money or resources. For example, Katrina's job at a frozen yogurt store requires her to keep track of how much of each flavor of yogurt is left. She notices that there is always peanut butter yogurt left over, but the raspberry is always running low. She realizes that the amounts of yogurt that are ordered need to be adjusted. The store's resources are not being used effectively: They are spending the same amount on peanut butter and raspberry yogurt, while the raspberry yogurt sells out and the peanut butter yogurt goes to waste. Katrina told the manager that she thought that he should reconsider how he spent his ordering dollars. When she gave him the evidence, he agreed and thanked her for the tip. When Katrina moved to a new city, he also gave her a glowing recommendation that helped her land a great new job.

People who are self-employed also use business budgets. A house painter uses a budget to determine costs for a job. If too much money is spent on supplies and the job runs over budget, the painter will not show a profit and will soon be out of business.

The steps for a basic business budget are similar to those of a basic personal budget. They are:

1. Determining and/or understanding a business plan.
2. Estimating costs.
3. Establishing prices.
4. Estimating volume of business.

To understand how to create a business budget, follow the steps that Ariel takes as she starts a typing service.

Understanding Business Plans

A business plan is an outline of the goals of a business. Business plans detail what products or services are to be supplied and how much money and resources will be needed. Self-employed people make their own business plans. People who are employed by others may not necessarily know much about the company's business plan, but they need to understand its goals in order to succeed in their jobs.

Ariel plans to start a typing service in six months when the fall school semester begins. Her business goal is to provide typing services to local high school and college students on a part-time basis. The business plan that she created covers what she expects from the first and second year of business.

Ariel's Business Plan

Year One

September through December: Establish clients through advertising and coupons placed around the two schools that are near Ariel's home. To track advertising success, Ariel will ask all customers how they learned about her services.

January through May: Increase the number of clients by 10 percent over the previous period. Ariel also expects typing revenues to increase by this amount. She will use the advertising that was successful in the first four months. She will also offer discounts to current clients who refer their friends to her typing service.

June through August: Summer vacation.
Year Two

September through December: Graphics and color printing added to the list of services available. Posters advertise the new services.

January through May: Plan to increase business during the spring semester. During mid-term exams, the typing service will offer discounts to clients who have used the service before, and will distribute a coupon to mid-term customers to be used during the final exam period.

June through August: Summer vacation.

By making a long-term business plan, Ariel can set up a plan to accomplish immediate and future goals. This way, she knows what will happen at every step of her business's process. She can adequately plan her expenses to match her projected earnings—balancing her budget in advance. If Ariel sticks to the long-term plan she has made, she can achieve all of the goals she has set.

Estimating Costs
Some businesses and jobs cost very little to run. Baby-sitting requires few costs. The baby-sitter

Starting your own business, such as a lawn-mowing service, will require you to balance expenses against income.

needs only transportation to the job. Others, such as carpet cleaning, have higher costs. Carpet cleaners require special equipment, cleaning supplies, and transportation for their equipment.

Not all business costs are alike. To estimate the costs of running a business, a budget must divide costs into two categories: fixed costs and variable costs.

Fixed costs are business expenses that do not change, or that change very little, from month to month. A permanent fixed cost is an expense you expect to pay only once. Materials and equipment needed to run a business are considered fixed costs: equipment specific to the business (such as a carpet cleaning machine for a carpet cleaner), and office equipment are examples. Telephone bills and advertising expenses may be considered fixed costs if they are constant from month to month.

Variable costs are expenses that change from month to month, depending on the volume of business. In other words, variable costs depend on the number of products you sell or the number of customers you have.

For example, cleaning fluids for the carpet cleaner are variable costs. This is because the amount that a business uses in a month depends on the number of customers they have that month. The ice cream that a restaurant orders is also a variable cost—the amount varies from month to month based on the amount of ice cream that is consumed.

The following list divides expected costs for Ariel's typing service:

Fixed Costs Per Month	
Office supplies	$ 5.00
Advertising	$10.00
Permanent Fixed Costs	
Electric typewriter	$200.00
Variable Costs Per Customer	
Typing paper	$.03/sheet

In this way, Ariel is able to figure out how much it costs to run her business.

Establishing Prices

After a company or business person determines how much it costs to conduct business, a price must be set for the services or product. There are two common methods for setting prices.

The first method is to base prices on what competing businesses charge. For example, when she was starting her typing service, Ariel would call other established typing services to see what they charge. When comparing businesses and prices charged, it is important to make sure that the busi-

Understanding how to balance your business budget will help you achieve your long-term financial goals, like purchasing a car.

nesses are identical. Some typing services use computers, and some use electric typewriters.

The second method considers costs and what profit is desired. If Ariel were to choose this method for setting prices, she would answer the following questions:

Question 1. How much do you want to earn per hour? This is an estimate of an "hourly wage."

Question 2. How long does it take to complete each job, make each product, or service each customer?

Question 3. What are the total variable costs per customer? (This amount was determined in the previous budget step.)

Armed with answers to these questions, the typist

would be able to set prices for the new typing service by using the following formula:

      ____ Hours per customer (answer #2)
    × multiplied by
      ____ Hourly wage (answer #1)
    = equals
      ____ Total wage

Total wage would then be added to total variable costs (answer #3).

      ____ Total wage
    + plus
      ____ Total variable costs (answer #3)
    = equals
      ____ Price

Then, the typist would divide that price by the number of hours per customer (answer #2) to determine the hourly price of the new typing service.

      ____ Price
    ÷ divided by
      ____ Hours per customer (answer #2)
    = equals
      ____ Hourly price

Estimating Expected Volume of Business

The final step of building a business budget is to estimate how much business is expected. The level of activity a business shows may vary from month to month. Some businesses don't show a profit every month, and their budgets should reflect this. But if a business should earn a certain amount of money each month and does not do so, the budget can be adjusted, often before the company is in trouble.

Ariel does not plan to work during the summer months. Since she has planned for this time off, her expected volume of business will be zero for three months of the year.

Putting It All Together

Organizing a business budget takes thought and energy, but it is essential for starting or maintaining a business. Ariel's typing service now has a business budget and is ready for business.

Just as with personal budgets, business budgets require updating and adjustment. Price changes for variable costs, increased competition, and growth of a business all require budget adjustments.

Consider some of Ariel's budget decisions as she plans to enter her third year running the typing service:

• Last year, another new typing service advertised at

the local college. Ariel considers this new service to be in direct competition with her. The new service offered the same prices as Ariel's, but they spent more on advertising. Ariel decides to increase her level of advertising and take out an ad in the college newspaper. This will become a new variable cost for the typing service budget.

- Ariel wants to expand her business to include desktop publishing, but that requires a computer and a high-quality printer. She finds that she can rent time on a computer at the local copy shop, which will save her the expense of having to buy a computer. The copy shop can also print what she produces on the computer. She will have to add the rental expense to the cost area of her budget and establish a price for the service. She also expects that the new service will increase her volume of business and is considering working during the summer months if the demand is high enough.

If you make the effort to learn good budgeting habits, you will be able to apply them to your place of work. Like Ariel, you can set long-range plans so that you can achieve your greater goals. Or, like Katrina, your budgeting skills could win you the respect of your boss. Regardless of what kind of job you have, budgeting skills will help you get ahead.

You can experience the positive effects now and in your future career.

Questions to Ask Yourself

Understanding budgets is a vital workplace skill, whether you work for a large company or run your own business. 1) How can business people budget human resources? 2) How is a business budget like a personal budget? 3) What kinds of costs must a business plan to meet?

Budgeting for Future Success

TODAY'S WORLD AND WORKPLACE ARE CONSIDERED a "global village." Telecommunications and air transportation make finance, technology, and labor available to a world economy. As the year 2000 approaches, increased knowledge and skills will be required to compete in the changing workplace created by the world economy.

To be prepared for a career in the next century, people will need a variety of skills. The use of budgets is one such necessary skill. Allocating money, solving problems, and making decisions are skills needed to create and use either a personal or business budget. These skills are also critical for people who want to be ready to achieve personal and professional success.

If you learn good budgeting skills and are able to apply them to different situations, people will take notice. At your current job, you can impress your employer by suggesting possible budgeting improvements. If you help your boss now, he or she will

Budgeting your money carefully will help you save for things you really want.

help you later. Maybe your boss will write you a good recommendation for a future job, as Katrina's manager did in chapter 3. Or perhaps he or she will help you find a good job when you finish school. Whatever the case, using your budgeting skills now can only benefit you in your future career.

You will also find that balancing your current budget, no matter how little money it may involve, will help you balance your personal budget in the future. You will be making more money when you begin your career, but balancing your budget then will involve the same steps that it does now. That way, when you do begin to earn more money—and possibly even have to balance a budget that includes a spouse and children—you will be well prepared to do it.

Success with budgets *can* be achieved. Many people start with basic personal budgets when learning to budget money. Tracking budget items and adjusting the budget over time gives experience that can be used with more complex budgets. Budgeting your allowance prepares you to budget when you have income from a job, for example. And budgeting part-time earnings prepares you to budget for your own business someday.

A budget may not make you rich. But when used with creativity, budgets can provide a sound basis on which to make decisions that will be easy to live with.

Questions to Ask Yourself

Good budgeting skills will get you noticed in the highly competitive workplace. 1) How can knowledge of budgeting help you in your career? 2) Would budgeting help you if you owned your own business? 3) Would a budget be useful if you had a family of your own?

Glossary

allocate To set something aside for a special purpose.

balanced budget Budget in which the amount of money received or earned is equal to or greater than the amount of money spent.

budget Plan that helps control how and where money is spent; a financial map.

business plan Written outline of a business idea including money needed, goals, and a plan to reach those goals.

debt An obligation or liability to pay something to someone else.

discretionary income The amount of money left over after all necessities are paid for.

expense Money spent by a person or business.

financial goal Something that you plan to do with your money, such as buy a car.

fixed expenses Expenses that are the same each month.

income Money that you earn or that is given to you, most commonly for doing some kind of work; the profit a business earns.

long-term goals Tasks you want to accomplish within a long period of time—a week, a month, or a year.

luxuries Items that you can live without.

necessities Items that you cannot live without; food is a necessity.

optional expenses Expenses that change each month.

profit The amount of money earned in a business after the costs of producing and selling its product are paid.

short-term goals Tasks you want to accomplish within a short period of time—today, tomorrow, or in a few days.

spending power Extra money that one has the power to spend as one chooses.

Organizations to Contact

THE FUTURE BUSINESS LEADERS OF AMERICA offers services that promote self-confidence, leadership, and business skills such as budgeting. Contact the national headquarters to find out if a local chapter exists in your area. For further information, write: P.O. Box 17417-Dulles, Washington, DC 20041; or call: 703-860-3334.

The U.S. Small Business Administration (SBA) offers programs and services to help business people with budgets. The SBA can provide training, educational programs, publications, and advice.

The SBA has offices around the country. Look in the telephone directory under "U.S. Government" to find the office nearest you. You may also call: 1-800-8-ASK-SBA.

The Consumer Credit Counseling Service (CCCS) provides services to individuals who are struggling with debt and personal budgeting problems. This nonprofit organization's services include helping people create personal budgets and negotiating with creditors. Look in the telephone directory in the white pages business section. CCCS has offices in most major cities.

For Further Reading

Barkin, Carol. *Jobs for Kids*. New York: Lothrop, Lee, and Shepard Books, 1990.

Berry, Joy. *Every Kid's Guide to Making and Managing Money*. Chicago: Children's Press, 1987.

Clark, Betty. *Coping on a Tight Budget*. New York: The Rosen Publishing Group, 1990.

Corrigan, Arnold, and Kaufman, Phyllis. *How to Use Credit and Credit Cards*. Stamford, CT: Longmeadow Press, 1987.

Godfrey, Neale. *Money Doesn't Grow on Trees*. New York: Simon & Schuster, 1994.

Hurwitz, Sue. *Careers Inside the World of Entrepreneurs*. New York: Rosen Publishing Group, 1995.

Klasky, Charles. *Budgeting*. Belmont, CA: David S. Lake Publishers, 1983.

Kyte, Kathleen S. *The Kids' Complete Guide to Money*. New York: Alfred A. Knopf, 1984.

Lehwald, Edward and Hanley, Christina. *Personal Banking*. Stamford, CT: Longmeadow Press, 1990.

Nichols, Harwood. *Money Sense*. Washington, DC: Acropolis Books Ltd., 1988.

Riehm, Sarah. *The Teenage Entrepreneur's Guide.* Chicago: Surrey Books, 1990.

Schmitt, Lois. *Smart Spending: A Young Consumer's Guide.* New York: Charles Scribner's Sons, 1989.

Weinstein, Grace. *The Lifetime Book of Money Management.* New York: New American Library, 1987.

Index

About the Author

Jane Hurwitz earned an M.A. in Economics from the University of Kansas. She has worked as a budget analyst for a large corporation. She is the coauthor of *Sally Ride, Shooting for the Stars, Staying Healthy,* and *Coping in a Blended Family.*

Photos

Cover by Matthew Baumann; all other photos by Matthew Baumann and Kim Sonsky.

Layout and Design

Kim Sonsky